POETRY
Death of a Naturalist
Door into the Dark
Wintering Out
North
Field Work
Poems 1965–1975
Sweeney Astray: A Version from the Irish
Station Island
The Haw Lantern
Selected Poems 1966–1987
Seeing Things
Sweeney's Flight (with photographs by Rachel Giese)
The Spirit Level

CRITICISM
Preoccupations: Selected Prose 1968–78
The Government of the Tongue
The Redress of Poetry
Crediting Poetry: The Nobel Lecture
Homage to Robert Frost (with Joseph Brodsky and Derek Walcott)

PLAYS
The Cure at Troy: A Version of Sophocles' Philoctetes

TRANSLATIONS
Laments: Poems of Jan Kochanowski (with Stanislaw Baranczak)

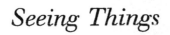

Seeing Things

SEEING

THINGS

SEAMUS

HEANEY

Farrar, Straus and Giroux
New York

Farrar, Straus and Giroux
18 West 18th Street, New York 10011

Copyright © 1991 by Seamus Heaney
All rights reserved
Printed in the United States of America
Originally published in 1991 by Faber and Faber Limited, Great Britain
First American edition published in 1991 by Farrar, Straus and Giroux
This edition first published in paperback in 1993

The Library of Congress has cataloged the hardcover edition as follows:
Heaney, Seamus, 1939–
Seeing things / Seamus Heaney. — 1st American ed.
p. cm.
ISBN: 978-0-374-52389-3
I. Title.

PR6058.E2S44   1991
821'.914—dc20

91021669

Paperback ISBN 978-0-374-52389-3

Designed by Cynthia Krupat

www.fsgbooks.com

P1

for Derek Mahon

Acknowledgements

Acknowledgements are due to the editors of
the following, where some of these poems
appeared for the first time: *Agenda*; *Agni
Review*; *Antaeus*; *Belfast Newsletter*; *English
Review*; *Field*; *Georgia Review*; *Irish Times*;
London Review of Books; *The Observer*; *Orbis*;
Owl; *Oxford Gazette*; *Oxford Poetry*; *Parnassus*;
Ploughshares; *Poetry Ireland*; *Poetry Review*;
Salmagundi; *Stet*; *Sunday Tribune*; *Thames
Poetry*; *The Threepenny Review*; *The Times
Literary Supplement*; *Tikkun*; *Translation*.
The following were first published by
The New Yorker: 'A Basket of Chestnuts',
'Squarings', Nos. xviii, xxx, xxxi, xxxii, xxxiii,
xxxiv, xxxv, xxxvi.
A number of the poems in Part I were printed
in *The Tree Clock* (Linen Hall Library,
Belfast, 1990).
Acknowledgement is due to John Montague for
the quotation from "The Water Carrier" on
page 52.

Contents

PART II/SQUARINGS

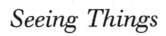

Seeing Things

The Golden Bough

(*Aeneid*, Book VI, lines 98–148)

So from the back of her shrine the Sibyl of Cumae
Chanted fearful equivocal words and made the cave echo
With sayings where clear truths and mysteries
Were inextricably twined. Apollo turned and twisted
His spurs at her breast, gave her her head, then reined
    in her spasms.

As soon as her fit passed away and the mad mouthings
    stopped,
Heroic Aeneas began: 'No ordeal, O Priestess,
That you can imagine would ever surprise me,
For already I have foreseen and foresuffered all.
But one thing I pray for especially: since they say it is
    here
That the King of the Underworld's gateway is to be found,
Among these shadowy marshes where Acheron comes
    flooding through,
I pray for one look, one face-to-face meeting with my
    dear father.
Teach me the way and open the holy doors wide.
I carried him on these shoulders through flames
And thousands of enemy spears. In the thick of battle I
    saved him
And he was at my side then through all my sea-journeys,
A man in old age, worn out yet holding out always.
And he too it was who half-prayed and half-ordered me

3

To make this approach, to find and petition you.
So therefore, Vestal, I beseech you take pity
On a son and a father, for nothing is out of your power
Whom Hecate appointed the keeper of wooded Avernus.
If Orpheus could call back the shade of a wife through
    his faith
In the loudly plucked strings of his Thracian lyre,
If Pollux could redeem a brother by going in turns
Backwards and forwards so often to the land of the dead,
And if Theseus too, and great Hercules . . . But why
    speak of them?
I myself am of highest birth, a descendant of Jove.'

He was praying like that and holding on to the altar
When the prophetess started to speak: 'Blood relation of
    gods,
Trojan, son of Anchises, the way down to Avernus is easy.
Day and night black Pluto's door stands open.
But to retrace your steps and get back to upper air,
This is the real task and the real undertaking.
A few have been able to do it, sons of gods
Favoured by Jupiter the Just, or exalted to heaven
In a blaze of heroic glory. Forests spread midway down,
And Cocytus winds through the dark, licking its banks.
Still, if love torments you so much and you so much need
To sail the Stygian lake twice and twice to inspect

The murk of Tartarus, if you will go beyond the limit,
Understand what you must do beforehand.
Hidden in the thick of a tree is a bough made of gold
And its leaves and pliable twigs are made of it too.
It is sacred to underworld Juno, who is its patron,
And it is roofed in by a grove, where deep shadows mass
Along far wooded valleys. No one is ever permitted
To go down to earth's hidden places unless he has first
Plucked this golden-fledged growth out of its tree
And handed it over to fair Proserpina, to whom it belongs
By decree, her own special gift. And when it is plucked,
A second one always grows in its place, golden again,
And the foliage growing on it has the same metal sheen.
Therefore look up and search deep and when you have
    found it
Take hold of it boldly and duly. If fate has called you,
The bough will come away easily, of its own accord.
Otherwise, no matter how much strength you muster,
    you never will
Manage to quell it or cut it down with the toughest of
    blades.'

PART I

The Journey Back

Larkin's shade surprised me. He quoted Dante:

'*Daylight was going and the umber air*
Soothing every creature on the earth,
Freeing them from their labours everywhere.

I alone was girding myself to face
The ordeal of my journey and my duty
And not a thing had changed, as rush-hour buses

Bore the drained and laden through the city.
I might have been a wise king setting out
Under the Christmas lights—except that

It felt more like the forewarned journey back
Into the heartland of the ordinary.
Still my old self. Ready to knock one back.

A nine-to-five man who had seen poetry.'

Markings

I

We marked the pitch: four jackets for four goalposts,
That was all. The corners and the squares
Were there like longitude and latitude
Under the bumpy ground, to be
Agreed about or disagreed about
When the time came. And then we picked the teams
And crossed the line our called names drew between us.

Youngsters shouting their heads off in a field
As the light died and they kept on playing
Because by then they were playing in their heads
And the actual kicked ball came to them
Like a dream heaviness, and their own hard
Breathing in the dark and skids on grass
Sounded like effort in another world . . .
It was quick and constant, a game that never need
Be played out. Some limit had been passed,
There was fleetness, furtherance, untiredness
In time that was extra, unforeseen and free.

II

You also loved lines pegged out in the garden,
The spade nicking the first straight edge along
The tight white string. Or string stretched perfectly
To mark the outline of a house foundation,

Pale timber battens set at right angles
For every corner, each freshly sawn new board
Spick and span in the oddly passive grass.
Or the imaginary line straight down
A field of grazing, to be ploughed open
From the rod stuck in one headrig to the rod
Stuck in the other.

III

All these things entered you
As if they were both the door and what came through it.
They marked the spot, marked time and held it open.
A mower parted the bronze sea of corn.
A windlass hauled the centre out of water.
Two men with a cross-cut kept it swimming
Into a felled beech backwards and forwards
So that they seemed to row the steady earth.

Three Drawings

Those were the days—
booting a leather football
truer and farther
than you ever expected!

It went rattling
hard and fast
over daisies and benweeds,
it thumped

but it sang too,
a kind of dry, ringing
foreclosure of sound.
Or else, a great catch

and a cry from the touch-line
to *Point her!* That spring
and unhampered smash-through!
Was it you

or the ball that kept going
beyond you, amazingly
higher and higher
and ruefully free?

2. THE PULSE

The effortlessness
of a spinning reel. One quick
flick of the wrist
and your minnow sped away

whispering and silky
and nimbly laden.
It seemed to be all rise
and shine, the very opposite

of uphill going—it was pure
duration, and when it ended,
the pulse of the cast line
entering water

was smaller in your hand
than the remembered heartbeat
of a bird. Then, after all of that
runaway give, you were glad

when you reeled in and found
yourself strung, heel-tip
to rod-tip, into the river's
steady purchase and thrum.

3 . A HAUL

The one that got away
from Thor and the giant Hymir
was the world-serpent itself.
The god had baited his line

with an ox-head, spun it high
and plunged it into the depths.
But the big haul came to an end
when Thor's foot went through the boards

and Hymir panicked and cut
the line with a bait-knife. Then
roll-over, turmoil, whiplash!
A Milky Way in the water.

The hole he smashed in the boat
opened, the way Thor's head
opened out there on the sea.
He felt at one with space,

unroofed and obvious—
surprised in his empty arms
like some fabulous high-catcher
coming down without the ball.

Casting and Gathering

for Ted Hughes

Years and years ago, these sounds took sides:

On the left bank, a green silk tapered cast
Went whispering through the air, saying *hush*
And *lush*, entirely free, no matter whether
It swished above the hayfield or the river.

On the right bank, like a speeded-up corncrake,
A sharp ratcheting went on and on
Cutting across the stillness as another
Fisherman gathered line-lengths off his reel.

I am still standing there, awake and dreamy,
I have grown older and can see them both
Moving their arms and rods, working away,
Each one absorbed, proofed by the sounds he's making.

One sound is saying, 'You are not worth tuppence,
But neither is anybody. Watch it! Be severe.'
The other says, 'Go with it! Give and swerve.
You are everything you feel beside the river.'

I love hushed air. I trust contrariness.
Years and years go past and I do not move
For I see that when one man casts, the other gathers
And then *vice versa*, without changing sides.

Man and Boy

'Catch the old one first'
(My father's joke was also old, and heavy
And predictable), 'then the young ones
Will all follow, and Bob's your uncle.'

On slow bright river evenings, the sweet time
Made him afraid we'd take too much for granted
And so our spirits must be lightly checked.

Blessed be down-to-earth! Blessed be highs!
Blessed be the detachment of dumb love
In that broad-backed, low-set man
Who feared debt all his life, but now and then
Could make a splash like the salmon he said was
'As big as a wee pork pig by the sound of it'.

II

In earshot of the pool where the salmon jumped
Back through its own unheard concentric soundwaves
A mower leans forever on his scythe.

He has mown himself to the centre of the field
And stands in a final perfect ring
Of sunlit stubble.

'Go and tell your father,' the mower says
(He said it to my father who told me),
'I have it mowed as clean as a new sixpence.'

My father is a barefoot boy with news,
Running at eye-level with weeds and stooks
On the afternoon of his own father's death.

The open, black half of the half-door waits.
I feel much heat and hurry in the air.
I feel his legs and quick heels far away

And strange as my own—when he will piggyback me
At a great height, light-headed and thin-boned,
Like a witless elder rescued from the fire.

Seeing Things

Inishbofin on a Sunday morning.
Sunlight, turfsmoke, seagulls, boatslip, diesel.
One by one we were being handed down
Into a boat that dipped and shilly-shallied
Scaresomely every time. We sat tight
On short cross-benches, in nervous twos and threes,
Obedient, newly close, nobody speaking
Except the boatmen, as the gunwales sank
And seemed they might ship water any minute.
The sea was very calm but even so,
When the engine kicked and our ferryman
Swayed for balance, reaching for the tiller,
I panicked at the shiftiness and heft
Of the craft itself. What guaranteed us—
That quick response and buoyancy and swim—
Kept me in agony. All the time
As we went sailing evenly across
The deep, still, seeable-down-into water,
It was as if I looked from another boat
Sailing through air, far up, and could see
How riskily we fared into the morning,
And loved in vain our bare, bowed, numbered heads.

Claritas. The dry-eyed Latin word
Is perfect for the carved stone of the water
Where Jesus stands up to his unwet knees
And John the Baptist pours out more water
Over his head: all this in bright sunlight
On the façade of a cathedral. Lines
Hard and thin and sinuous represent
The flowing river. Down between the lines
Little antic fish are all go. Nothing else.
And yet in that utter visibility
The stone's alive with what's invisible:
Waterweed, stirred sand-grains hurrying off,
The shadowy, unshadowed stream itself.
All afternoon, heat wavered on the steps
And the air we stood up to our eyes in wavered
Like the zigzag hieroglyph for life itself.

III

Once upon a time my undrowned father
Walked into our yard. He had gone to spray
Potatoes in a field on the riverbank
And wouldn't bring me with him. The horse-sprayer
Was too big and newfangled, bluestone might
Burn me in the eyes, the horse was fresh, I
Might scare the horse, and so on. I threw stones
At a bird on the shed roof, as much for
The clatter of the stones as anything,
But when he came back, I was inside the house
And saw him out the window, scatter-eyed
And daunted, strange without his hat,
His step unguided, his ghosthood immanent.
When he was turning on the riverbank,
The horse had rusted and reared up and pitched
Cart and sprayer and everything off balance,
So the whole rig went over into a deep
Whirlpool, hoofs, chains, shafts, cartwheels, barrel
And tackle, all tumbling off the world,
And the hat already merrily swept along
The quieter reaches. That afternoon
I saw him face to face, he came to me
With his damp footprints out of the river,
And there was nothing between us there
That might not still be happily ever after.

The Ash Plant

He'll never rise again but he is ready.
Entered like a mirror by the morning,
He stares out the big window, wondering,
Not caring if the day is bright or cloudy.

An upstairs outlook on the whole country.
First milk-lorries, first smoke, cattle, trees
In damp opulence above damp hedges—
He has it to himself, he is like a sentry

Forgotten and unable to remember
The whys and wherefores of his lofty station,
Wakening relieved yet in position,
Disencumbered as a breaking comber.

As his head goes light with light, his wasting hand
Gropes desperately and finds the phantom limb
Of an ash plant in his grasp, which steadies him.
Now he has found his touch he can stand his ground

Or wield the stick like a silver bough and come
Walking again among us: the quoted judge.
I could have cut a better man out of the hedge!
God might have said the same, remembering Adam.

I.I.87

Dangerous pavements.
But I face the ice this year
With my father's stick.

An August Night

His hands were warm and small and knowledgeable.
When I saw them again last night, they were two ferrets,
Playing all by themselves in a moonlit field.

Field of Vision

I remember this woman who sat for years
In a wheelchair, looking straight ahead
Out the window at sycamore trees unleafing
And leafing at the far end of the lane.

Straight out past the TV in the corner,
The stunted, agitated hawthorn bush,
The same small calves with their backs to wind and rain,
The same acre of ragwort, the same mountain.

She was steadfast as the big window itself.
Her brow was clear as the chrome bits of the chair.
She never lamented once and she never
Carried a spare ounce of emotional weight.

Face to face with her was an education
Of the sort you got across a well-braced gate—
One of those lean, clean, iron, roadside ones
Between two whitewashed pillars, where you could see

Deeper into the country than you expected
And discovered that the field behind the hedge
Grew more distinctly strange as you kept standing
Focused and drawn in by what barred the way.

The Pitchfork

Of all implements, the pitchfork was the one
That came near to an imagined perfection:
When he tightened his raised hand and aimed with it,
It felt like a javelin, accurate and light.

So whether he played the warrior or the athlete
Or worked in earnest in the chaff and sweat,
He loved its grain of tapering, dark-flecked ash
Grown satiny from its own natural polish.

Riveted steel, turned timber, burnish, grain,
Smoothness, straightness, roundness, length and sheen.
Sweat-cured, sharpened, balanced, tested, fitted.
The springiness, the clip and dart of it.

And then when he thought of probes that reached the
    farthest,
He would see the shaft of a pitchfork sailing past
Evenly, imperturbably through space,
Its prongs starlit and absolutely soundless—

But has learned at last to follow that simple lead
Past its own aim, out to an other side
Where perfection—or nearness to it—is imagined
Not in the aiming but the opening hand.

A Basket of Chestnuts

There's a shadow-boost, a giddy strange assistance
That happens when you swing a loaded basket.
The lightness of the thing seems to diminish
The actual weight of what's being hoisted in it.

For a split second your hands feel unburdened,
Outstripped, dismayed, passed through.
Then just as unexpectedly comes rebound—
Downthrust and comeback ratifying you.

I recollect this basket full of chestnuts,
A really solid gather-up, all drag
And lustre, opulent and gravid
And golden-bowelled as a moneybag.

And I wish they could be painted, known for what
Pigment might see beyond them, what the reach
Of sense despairs of as it fails to reach it,
Especially the thwarted sense of touch.

Since Edward Maguire visited our house
In the autumn of 1973,
A basketful of chestnuts shines between us,
One that he did not paint when he painted me—

Although it was what he thought he'd maybe use
As a decoy or a coffer for the light
He captured in the toecaps of my shoes.
But it wasn't in the picture and is not.

What's there is comeback, especially for him.
In oils and brushwork we are ratified.
And the basket shines and foxfire chestnuts gleam
Where he passed through, unburdened and dismayed.

The Biretta

Like Gaul, the biretta was divided
Into three parts: triple-finned black serge,
A shipshape pillbox, its every slope and edge
Trimly articulated and decided.

Its insides were crimped satin; it was heavy too
But sported a light flossy tassel
That the backs of my fingers remember well,
And it left a dark red line on the priest's brow.

I received it into my hand from the hand
Of whoever was celebrant, one thin
Fastidious movement up and out and in
In the name of the Father and of the Son AND

Of the Holy Ghost . . . I placed it on the steps
Where it seemed to batten down, even half-resist
All of the brisk proceedings of the Mass—
The chalice drunk off and the patted lips.

The first time I saw one, I heard a shout
As an El Greco ascetic rose before me
Preaching hellfire, saurian and stormy,
Adze-head on the rampage in the pulpit.

Sanctuaries. Marble. Kneeling boards. Vocation.
Some it made look squashed, some clean and tall.
It was antique as armour in a hall
And put the wind up me and my generation.

Now I turn it upside down and it is a boat—
A paper boat, or the one that wafts into
The first lines of the *Purgatorio*
As poetry lifts its eyes and clears its throat.

Or maybe that small boat out of the Bronze Age
Where the oars are needles and the worked gold frail
As the intact half of a hatched-out shell,
Refined beyond the dross into sheer image.

But in the end it's as likely to be the one
In Matthew Lawless's painting *The Sick Call*,
Where the scene is out on a river and it's all
Solid, pathetic and Irish Victorian.

In which case, however, his reverence wears a hat.
Undaunting, half-domestic, loved in crises,
He sits listening as each long oar dips and rises,
Sad for his worthy life and fit for it.

The Settle Bed

Willed down, waited for, in place at last and for good.
Trunk-hasped, cart-heavy, painted an ignorant brown.
And pew-strait, bin-deep, standing four-square as an ark.

If I lie in it, I am cribbed in seasoned deal
Dry as the unkindled boards of a funeral ship.
My measure has been taken, my ear shuttered up.

Yet I hear an old sombre tide awash in the headboard:
Unpathetic *och ochs* and *och hohs*, the long bedtime
Anthems of Ulster, unwilling, unbeaten,

Protestant, Catholic, the Bible, the beads,
Long talks at gables by moonlight, boots on the hearth,
The small hours chimed sweetly away so next thing it
     was

The cock on the ridge-tiles.
                    And now this is 'an inheritance'—
Upright, rudimentary, unshiftably planked
In the long ago, yet willable forward

Again and again and again, cargoed with
Its own dumb, tongue-and-groove worthiness
And un-get-roundable weight. But to conquer that
     weight,

Imagine a dower of settle beds tumbled from heaven
Like some nonsensical vengeance on the people,
Then learn from that harmless barrage that whatever is
   given

Can always be reimagined, however four-square,
Plank-thick, hull-stupid and out of its time
It happens to be. You are free as the lookout,

That far-seeing joker posted high over the fog,
Who declared by the time that he had got himself down
The actual ship had been stolen away from beneath him.

The Schoolbag

in memoriam John Hewitt

My handsewn leather schoolbag. Forty years.
Poet, you were *nel mezzo del cammin*
When I shouldered it, half-full of blue-lined jotters,
And saw the classroom charts, the displayed bean,

The wallmap with its spray of shipping lanes
Describing arcs across the blue North Channel . . .
And in the middle of the road to school,
Ox-eye daisies and wild dandelions.

Learning's easy carried! The bag is light,
Scuffed and supple and unemptiable
As an itinerant school conjuror's hat.
So take it, for a word-hoard and a handsel,

As you step out trig and look back all at once
Like a child on his first morning leaving parents.

Glanmore Revisited

I. SCRABBLE

in memoriam Tom Delaney, archaeologist

Bare flags. Pump water. Winter-evening cold.
Our backs might never warm up but our faces
Burned from the hearth-blaze and the hot whiskeys.
It felt remembered even then, an old
Rightness half-imagined or foretold,
As green sticks hissed and spat into the ashes
And whatever rampaged out there couldn't reach us,
Firelit, shuttered, slated and stone-walled.

Year after year, our game of Scrabble: love
Taken for granted like any other word
That was chanced on and allowed within the rules.
So 'scrabble' let it be. Intransitive.
Meaning to scratch or rake at something hard.
Which is what he hears. Our scraping, clinking tools.

2. THE COT

Scythe and axe and hedge-clippers, the shriek
Of the gate the children used to swing on,
Poker, scuttle, tongs, a gravel rake—
The old activity starts up again
But starts up differently. We're on our own
Years later in the same *locus amoenus*,
Tenants no longer, but in full possession
Of an emptied house and whatever keeps between us.

Which must be more than keepsakes, even though
The child's cot's back in place where Catherine
Woke in the dawn and answered *doodle doo*
To the rooster in the farm across the road—
And is the same cot I myself slept in
When the whole world was a farm that eked and crowed.

3. SCENE SHIFTS

Only days after a friend had cut his name
Into the ash, our kids stripped off the bark—
The first time I was really angry at them.
I was flailing round the house like a man berserk
And maybe overdoing it, although
The business had moved me at the time;
It brought back those blood-brother scenes where two
Braves nick wrists and cross them for a sign.

Where it shone like bone exposed is healed up now.
The bark's thick-eared and welted with a scar—
Like the hero's in a recognition scene
In which old nurse sees old wound, then clasps brow
(Astonished at what all this starts to mean)
And tears surprise the veteran of the war.

4 · 1973

The corrugated iron growled like thunder
When March came in; then as the year turned warmer
And invalids and bulbs came up from under,
I hibernated on behind the dormer,
Staring through shaken branches at the hill,
Dissociated, like an ailing farmer
Chloroformed against things seasonal
In a reek of cigarette smoke and dropped ash.

Lent came in next, also like a lion
Sinewy and wild for discipline,
A fasted will marauding through the body;
And I taunted it with scents of nicotine
As I lit one off another, and felt rash,
And stirred in the deep litter of the study.

5. LUSTRAL SONNET

Breaking and entering: from early on,
Words that thrilled me far more than they scared me—
And still did, when I came into my own
Masquerade as a man of property.
Even then, my first impulse was never
To double-bar a door or lock a gate;
And fitted blinds and curtains drawn over
Seemed far too self-protective and uptight.

But I scared myself when I re-entered here,
My own first breaker-in, with an instruction
To saw up the old bed-frame, since the stair
Was much too narrow for it. A bad action,
So Greek with consequence, so dangerous,
Only pure words and deeds secure the house.

6. BEDSIDE READING

The whole place airier. Big summer trees
Stirring at eye level when we waken
And little shoots of ivy creeping in
Unless they've been trained out—like memories
You've trained so long now they can show their face
And keep their distance. White-mouthed depression
Swims out from its shadow like a dolphin
With wet, unreadable, unfurtive eyes.

I swim in Homer. In Book Twenty-three.
At last Odysseus and Penelope
Waken together. One bedpost of the bed
Is the living trunk of an old olive tree
And is their secret. As ours could have been ivy,
Evergreen, atremble and unsaid.

7. THE SKYLIGHT

You were the one for skylights. I opposed
Cutting into the seasoned tongue-and-groove
Of pitch pine. I liked it low and closed,
Its claustrophobic, nest-up-in-the-roof
Effect. I liked the snuff-dry feeling,
The perfect, trunk-lid fit of the old ceiling.
Under there, it was all hutch and hatch.
The blue slates kept the heat like midnight thatch.

But when the slates came off, extravagant
Sky entered and held surprise wide open.
For days I felt like an inhabitant
Of that house where the man sick of the palsy
Was lowered through the roof, had his sins forgiven,
Was healed, took up his bed and walked away.

A Pillowed Head

Matutinal. Mother-of-pearl
Summer come early. Slashed carmines
And washed milky blues.

To be first on the road,
Up with the ground-mists and pheasants.
To be older and grateful

That this time you too were half-grateful
The pangs had begun—prepared
An. clear-headed, foreknowing

The trauma, entering on it
With full consent of the will.
(The first time, dismayed and arrayed

In your cut-off white cotton gown,
You were more bride than earth-mother
Up on the stirrup-rigged bed,

Who were self-possessed now
To the point of a walk on the pier
Before you checked in.)

And then later on I half-fainted
When the little slapped palpable girl
Was handed to me; but as usual

Came to in two wide-open eyes
That had been dawned into farther
Than ever, and had outseen the last

Of all those mornings of waiting
When your domed brow was one long held silence
And the dawn chorus anything but.

A Royal Prospect

On the day of their excursion up the Thames
To Hampton Court, they were nearly sunstruck.
She with her neck bared in a page-boy cut,
He all dreamy anyhow, wild for her
But pretending to be a thousand miles away,
Studying the boat's wake in the water.
And here are the photographs. Head to one side,
In her sleeveless blouse, one bare shoulder high
And one arm loose, a bird with a dropped wing
Surprised in cover. He looks at you straight,
Assailable, enamoured, full of vows,
Young dauphin in the once-upon-a-time.
And next the lowish red-brick Tudor frontage.
No more photographs, however, now
We are present there as the smell of grass
And suntan oil, standing like their sixth sense
Behind them at the entrance to the maze,
Heartbroken for no reason, willing them
To dare it to the centre they are lost for . . .
Instead, like reflections staggered through warped glass,
They reappear as in a black and white
Old grainy newsreel, where their pleasure-boat
Goes back spotlit across sunken bridges
And they alone are borne downstream unscathed,
Between mud banks where the wounded rave all night
At flameless blasts and echoless gunfire—

In all of which is ominously figured
Their free passage through historic times,
Like a silk train being brushed across a leper
Or the safe conduct of two royal favourites,
Unhindered and resented and bright-eyed.
So let them keep a tally of themselves
And be accountable when called upon,
For although by every golden mean their lot
Is fair and due, pleas will be allowed
Against every right and title vested in them
(And in a court where mere innocuousness
Has never gained approval or acquittal).

A Retrospect

The whole county apparently afloat:
Every road bridging or skirting water,
The land islanded, the field drains still as moats.

A bulrush sentried the lough shore: I had to
Wade barefoot over spongy, ice-cold marsh
(Soft bottom with bog water seeping through

The netted weeds) to get near where it stood
Perennially anomalous and dry,
Like chalk or velvet rooting in the mud.

Everything ran into water-colour.
The skyline was full up to the lip
As if the earth were going to brim over,

As if we moved in the first stealth of flood,
For remember, at one place, the swim and flow
From hidden springs made a river in the road.

Another trip they seemed to keep repeating
Was up to Glenshane Pass—his 'Trail of Tears',
As he'd say every time, and point out streams
He first saw on the road to boarding school.

And then he'd quote Sir John Davies' dispatch
About his progress through there from Dungannon
With Chichester in 1608:
'The wild inhabitants wondered as much
To see the King's deputy, as Virgil's ghosts
Wondered to see Aeneas alive in Hell.'

They liked the feel of the valley out behind,
As if a ladder leaned against the world
And they were climbing it but might fall back
Into the total air and emptiness
They carried on their shoulders.

               The old road
Went up and up, it was lover country,
Their drive-in in the sky, where each parked car
Played possum in the twilight and clouds moved
Smokily in the deep of polished roofs
And dormant windscreens.

              And there they were,
Astray in the hill-fort of all pleasures
Where air was other breath and grass a whisper,
Feeling empowered but still somehow constrained:
Young marrieds, used now to the licit within doors,
They fell short of the sweetness that had lured them.

No nest in rushes, the heather bells unbruised,
The love-drink of the mountain streams untasted.

So when they turned, they turned with the fasted eyes
Of wild inhabitants, and parked in silence
A bit down from the summit, where the brae
Swept off like a balcony, then seemed to drop
Sheer towards the baronies and cantreds.
Evening was dam water they saw down through.
The scene stood open, the visit lasted,
They gazed beyond themselves until he eased
The brake off and they freewheeled quickly
Before going into gear, with all their usual old
High-pitched strain and gradual declension.

The Rescue

In drifts of sleep I came upon you
Buried to your waist in snow.
You reached your arms out: I came to
Like water in a dream of thaw.

Wheels within Wheels

I

The first real grip I ever got on things
Was when I learned the art of pedalling
(By hand) a bike turned upside down, and drove
Its back wheel preternaturally fast.
I loved the disappearance of the spokes,
The way the space between the hub and rim
Hummed with transparency. If you threw
A potato into it, the hooped air
Spun mush and drizzle back into your face;
If you touched it with a straw, the straw frittered.
Something about the way those pedal treads
Worked very palpably at first against you
And then began to sweep your hand ahead
Into a new momentum—that all entered me
Like an access of free power, as if belief
Caught up and spun the objects of belief
In an orbit coterminous with longing.

II

But enough was not enough. Who ever saw
The limit in the given anyhow?
In fields beyond our house there was a well
('The well' we called it. It was more a hole
With water in it, with small hawthorn trees
On one side, and a muddy, dungy ooze

On the other, all tramped through by cattle).
I loved that too. I loved the turbid smell,
The sump-life of the place like old chain oil.
And there, next thing, I brought my bicycle.
I stood its saddle and its handlebars
Into the soft bottom, I touched the tyres
To the water's surface, then turned the pedals
Until like a mill-wheel pouring at the treadles
(But here reversed and lashing a mare's tail)
The world-refreshing and immersed back wheel
Spun lace and dirt-suds there before my eyes
And showered me in my own regenerate clays.
For weeks I made a nimbus of old glit.
Then the hub jammed, rims rusted, the chain snapped.

III

Nothing rose to the occasion after that
Until, in a circus ring, drumrolled and spotlit,
Cowgirls wheeled in, each one immaculate
At the still centre of a lariat.
Perpetuum mobile. Sheer pirouette.
Tumblers. Jongleurs. Ring-a-rosies. *Stet!*

The Sounds of Rain

in memoriam Richard Ellmann

I

An all-night drubbing overflow on boards
On the verandah. I dwelt without thinking
In the long moil of it, and then came to
To dripping eaves and light, saying into myself
Proven, weightless sayings of the dead.
Things like *He'll be missed* and *You'll have to thole.*

II

It could have been the drenched weedy gardens
Of Peredelkino: a reverie
Of looking out from late-winter gloom
Lit by tangerines and the clear of vodka,
Where Pasternak, lenient yet austere,
Answered for himself without insistence.

'I had the feeling of an immense debt,'
He said (it is recorded). 'So many years
Just writing lyric poetry and translating.
I felt there was some duty . . . Time was passing.
And with all its faults, it has more value
Than those early . . . It is richer, more humane.'

Or it could have been the thaw and puddles
Of Athens Street where William Alfred stood
On the wet doorstep, remembering the friend

Who died at sixty. 'After "Summer Tides"
There would have been a deepening, you know,
Something ampler . . . Ah well. Good night again.'

III

The eaves a water-fringe and steady lash
Of summer downpour: *You are steeped in luck*,
I hear them say, *Steeped, steeped, steeped in luck*.
And hear the flood too, gathering from under,
Biding and boding like a masterwork
Or a named name that overbrims itself.

Fosterling

'That heavy greenness fostered by water'

At school I loved one picture's heavy greenness—
Horizons rigged with windmills' arms and sails.
The millhouses' still outlines. Their in-placeness
Still more in place when mirrored in canals.
I can't remember never having known
The immanent hydraulics of a land
Of *glar* and *glit* and floods at *dailigone*.
My silting hope. My lowlands of the mind.

Heaviness of being. And poetry
Sluggish in the doldrums of what happens.
Me waiting until I was nearly fifty
To credit marvels. Like the tree-clock of tin cans
The tinkers made. So long for air to brighten,
Time to be dazzled and the heart to lighten.

PART II

SQUARINGS

1. Lightenings

Shifting brilliancies. Then winter light
In a doorway, and on the stone doorstep
A beggar shivering in silhouette.

So the particular judgement might be set:
Bare wallstead and a cold hearth rained into—
Bright puddle where the soul-free cloud-life roams.

And after the commanded journey, what?
Nothing magnificent, nothing unknown.
A gazing out from far away, alone.

And it is not particular at all,
Just old truth dawning: there is no next-time-round.
Unroofed scope. Knowledge-freshening wind.

Roof it again. Batten down. Dig in.
Drink out of tin. Know the scullery cold,
A latch, a door-bar, forged tongs and a grate.

Touch the cross-beam, drive iron in a wall,
Hang a line to verify the plumb
From lintel, coping-stone and chimney-breast.

Relocate the bedrock in the threshold.
Take squarings from the recessed gable pane.
Make your study the unregarded floor.

Sink every impulse like a bolt. Secure
The bastion of sensation. Do not waver
Into language. Do not waver in it.

iii

Squarings? In the game of marbles, squarings
Were all those anglings, aimings, feints and squints
You were allowed before you'd shoot, all those

Hunkerings, tensings, pressures of the thumb,
Test-outs and pull-backs, re-envisagings,
All the ways your arms kept hoping towards

Blind certainties that were going to prevail
Beyond the one-off moment of the pitch.
A million million accuracies passed

Between your muscles' outreach and that space
Marked with three round holes and a drawn line.
You squinted out from a skylight of the world.

iv

Beneath the ocean of itself, the crowd
In Roman theatres could hear another
Stronger groundswell coming through.

It was like the steady message in a shell
Held to the ear in earshot of the sea:
Words being spoken on the scene arrived

Resonating up through the walls of urns.
The cordoned air rolled back, wave upon wave
Of classic mouthfuls amplified and faded.

How airy and how earthed it felt up there,
Bare to the world, light-headed, volatile
And carried like the rests in tides or music.

Three marble holes thumbed in the concrete road
Before the concrete hardened still remained
Three decades after the marble-player vanished

Into Australia. Three stops to play
The music of the arbitrary on.
Blow on them now and hear an undersong

Your levelled breath made once going over
The empty bottle. Improvise. Make free
Like old hay in its flimsy afterlife

High on a windblown hedge. Ocarina earth.
Three listening posts up on some hard-baked tier
Above the resonating amphorae.

vi

Once, as a child, out in a field of sheep,
Thomas Hardy pretended to be dead
And lay down flat among their dainty shins.

In that sniffed-at, bleated-into, grassy space
He experimented with infinity.
His small cool brow was like an anvil waiting

For sky to make it sing the perfect pitch
Of his dumb being, and that stir he caused
In the fleece-hustle was the original

Of a ripple that would travel eighty years
Outward from there, to be the same ripple
Inside him at its last circumference.

vii

(I misremembered. He went down on all fours,
Florence Emily says, crossing a ewe-leaze.
Hardy sought the creatures face to face,

Their witless eyes and liability
To panic made him feel less alone,
Made proleptic sorrow stand a moment

Over him, perfectly known and sure.
And then the flock's dismay went swimming on
Into the blinks and murmurs and deflections

He'd know at parties in renowned old age
When sometimes he imagined himself a ghost
And circulated with that new perspective.)

viii

The annals say: when the monks of Clonmacnoise
Were all at prayers inside the oratory
A ship appeared above them in the air.

The anchor dragged along behind so deep
It hooked itself into the altar rails
And then, as the big hull rocked to a standstill,

A crewman shinned and grappled down the rope
And struggled to release it. But in vain.
'This man can't bear our life here and will drown,'

The abbot said, 'unless we help him.' So
They did, the freed ship sailed, and the man climbed
     back
Out of the marvellous as he had known it.

ix

A boat that did not rock or wobble once
Sat in long grass one Sunday afternoon
In nineteen forty-one or -two. The heat

Out on Lough Neagh and in where cattle stood
Jostling and skittering near the hedge
Grew redolent of the tweed skirt and tweed sleeve

I nursed on. I remember little treble
Timber-notes their smart heels struck from planks,
Me cradled in an elbow like a secret

Open now as the eye of heaven was then
Above three sisters talking, talking steady
In a boat the ground still falls and falls from under.

x

Overhang of grass and seedling birch
On the quarry face. Rock-hob where you watched
All that cargoed brightness travelling

Above and beyond and sumptuously across
The water in its clear deep dangerous holes
On the quarry floor. Ultimate

Fathomableness, ultimate
Stony up-againstness: could you reconcile
What was diaphanous there with what was massive?

Were you equal to or were you opposite
To build-ups so promiscuous and weightless?
Shield your eyes, look up and face the music.

xi

To put a glass roof on the handball alley
Where a hopped ball cut merciless angles
In and out of play, or levelled true

For the unanswerable dead-root . . .
He alone, our walking weathercock,
Our peeled eye at the easel, had the right

To make a studio of that free maze,
To turn light outside in and curb the space
Where accident got tricked to accuracy

And rain was rainier for being blown
Across the grid and texture of the concrete.
He scales the world at arm's length, gives thumbs up.

xii

And lightening? One meaning of that
Beyond the usual sense of alleviation,
Illumination, and so on, is this:

A phenomenal instant when the spirit flares
With pure exhilaration before death—
The good thief in us harking to the promise!

So paint him on Christ's right hand, on a promontory
Scanning empty space, so body-racked he seems
Untranslatable into the bliss

Ached for at the moon-rim of his forehead,
By nail-craters on the dark side of his brain:
This day thou shalt be with Me in Paradise.

2. Settings

Hazel stealth. A trickle in the culvert.
Athletic sea-light on the doorstep slab,
On the sea itself, on silent roofs and gables.

Whitewashed sun-traps. Hedges hot as chimneys.
Chairs on all fours. A plate-rack braced and laden.
The fossil poetry of hob and slate.

Desire within its moat, dozing at ease—
Like a gorged cormorant on the rock at noon,
Exiled and in tune with the big glitter.

Re-enter this as the adult of solitude,
The silence-forder and the definite
Presence you sensed withdrawing first time round.

xiv

One afternoon I was seraph on gold leaf.
I stood on the railway sleepers hearing larks,
Grasshoppers, cuckoos, dog-barks, trainer planes

Cutting and modulating and drawing off.
Heat wavered on the immaculate line
And shine of the cogged rails. On either side,

Dog daisies stood like vestals, the hot stones
Were clover-meshed and streaked with engine oil.
Air spanned, passage waited, the balance rode,

Nothing prevailed, whatever was in store
Witnessed itself already taking place
In a time marked by assent and by hiatus.

And strike this scene in gold too, in relief,
So that a greedy eye cannot exhaust it:
Stable straw, Rembrandt-gleam and burnish

Where my father bends to a tea-chest packed with salt,
The hurricane lamp held up at eye-level
In his bunched left fist, his right hand foraging

For the unbleeding, vivid-fleshed bacon,
Home-cured hocks pulled up into the light
For pondering awhile and putting back.

That night I owned the piled grain of Egypt.
I watched the sentry's torchlight on the hoard.
I stood in the door, unseen and blazed upon.

xvi

Rat-poison the colour of blood pudding
Went phosphorescent when it was being spread:
Its sparky rancid shine under the blade

Brought everything to life—like news of murder
Or the sight of a parked car occupied by lovers
On a side road, or stories of bull victims.

If a muse had sung the anger of Achilles
It would not have heightened the world-danger more.
It was all there in the fresh rat-poison

Corposant on mouldy, dried-up crusts.
On winter evenings I loved its reek and risk.
And windfalls freezing on the outhouse roof.

xvii

What were the virtues of an eelskin? What
Was the eel itself? A rib of water drawn
Out of the water, an ell yielded up

From glooms and whorls and slatings,
Rediscovered once it had been skinned.
When a wrist was bound with eelskin, energy

Redounded in that arm, a waterwheel
Turned in the shoulder, mill-races poured
And made your elbow giddy.

Your hand felt unconstrained and spirited
As heads and tails that wriggled in the mud
Aristotle supposed all eels were sprung from.

xviii

Like a foul-mouthed god of hemp come down to rut,
The rope-man stumped about and praised new rope
With talk of how thick it was, or how long and strong,

And how you could take it into your own hand
And feel it. His perfect, tight-bound wares
Made a circle round him: the makings of reins

And belly-bands and halters. And of slippage—
For even then, knee-high among the farmers,
I knew the rope-man menaced them with freedoms

They were going to turn their backs on; and knew too
His powerlessness once the fair-hill emptied
And he had to break the circle and start loading.

xix

Memory as a building or a city,
Well lighted, well laid out, appointed with
Tableaux vivants and costumed effigies—

Statues in purple cloaks, or painted red,
Ones wearing crowns, ones smeared with mud or blood:
So that the mind's eye could haunt itself

With fixed associations and learn to read
Its own contents in meaningful order,
Ancient textbooks recommended that

Familiar places be linked deliberately
With a code of images. You knew the portent
In each setting, you blinked and concentrated.

xx

On Red Square, the brick wall of the Kremlin
Looked unthreatening, in scale, just right for people
To behave well under, inside or outside.

The big cleared space in front was dizzying.
I looked across a heave and sweep of cobbles
Like the ones that beamed up in my dream of flying

Above the old cart road, with all the air
Fanning off beneath my neck and breastbone.
(The cloud-roamer, was it, Stalin called Pasternak?)

Terrible history and protected joys!
Plosive horse-dung on 1940s' roads.
The newsreel bomb-hits, as harmless as dust-puffs.

xxi

Once and only once I fired a gun—
A .22. At a square of handkerchief
Pinned on a tree about sixty yards away.

It exhilarated me—the bullet's song
So effortlessly at my fingertip,
The target's single shocking little jerk,

A whole new quickened sense of what *rifle* meant.
And then again as it was in the beginning
I saw the soul like a white cloth snatched away

Across dark galaxies and felt that shot
For the sin it was against eternal life—
Another phrase dilating in new light.

xxii

Where does spirit live? Inside or outside
Things remembed, made things, things unmade?
What came first, the seabird's cry or the soul

Imagined in the dawn cold when it cried?
Where does it roost at last? On dungy sticks
In a jackdaw's nest up in the old stone tower

Or a marble bust commanding the parterre?
How habitable is perfected form?
And how inhabited the windy light?

What's the use of a held note or held line
That cannot be assailed for reassurance?
(Set questions for the ghost of W.B.)

xxiii

On the bus-trip into saga country
Ivan Malinowski wrote a poem
About the nuclear submarines offshore

From an abandoned whaling station.
I remember it as a frisson, but cannot
Remember any words. What I wanted then

Was a poem of utter evening:
The thirteenth century, weird midnight sun
Setting at eye-level with Snorri Sturluson,

Who has come out to bathe in a hot spring
And sit through the stillness after milking time,
Laved and ensconced in the throne-room of his mind.

xxiv

Deserted harbour stillness. Every stone
Clarified and dormant under water,
The harbour wall a masonry of silence.

Fullness. Shimmer. Laden high Atlantic
The moorings barely stirred in, very slight
Clucking of the swell against boat boards.

Perfected vision: cockle minarets
Consigned down there with green-slicked bottle glass,
Shell-debris and a reddened bud of sandstone.

Air and ocean known as antecedents
Of each other. In apposition with
Omnipresence, equilibrium, brim.

3. Crossings

Travelling south at dawn, going full out
Through high-up stone-wall country, the rocks still cold,
Rain water gleaming here and there ahead,

I took a turn and met the fox stock-still,
Face-to-face in the middle of the road.
Wildness tore through me as he dipped and wheeled

In a level-running tawny breakaway.
O neat head, fabled brush and astonished eye
My blue Volkswagen flared into with morning!

Let rebirth come through water, through desire,
Through crawling backwards across clinic floors:
I have to cross back through that startled iris.

xxvi

Only to come up, year after year, behind
Those open-ended, canvas-covered trucks
Full of soldiers sitting cramped and staunch,

Their hands round gun-barrels, their gaze abroad
In dreams out of the body-heated metal.
Silent, time-proofed, keeping an even distance

Beyond the windscreen glass, carried ahead
On the phantasmal flow-back of the road,
They still mean business in the here and now.

So draw no attention, steer and concentrate
On the space that flees between like a speeded-up
Meltdown of souls from the straw-flecked ice of hell.

xxvii

Everything flows. Even a solid man,
A pillar to himself and to his trade,
All yellow boots and stick and soft felt hat,

Can sprout wings at the ankle and grow fleet
As the god of fair-days, stone posts, roads and crossroads,
Guardian of travellers and psychopomp.

'Look for a man with an ash plant on the boat,'
My father told his sister setting out
For London, 'and stay near him all night

And you'll be safe.' Flow on, flow on,
The journey of the soul with its soul guide
And the mysteries of dealing-men with sticks!

xxviii

The ice was like a bottle. We lined up
Eager to re-enter the long slide
We were bringing to perfection, time after time

Running and readying and letting go
Into a sheerness that was its own reward:
A farewell to surefootedness, a pitch

Beyond our usual hold upon ourselves.
And what went on kept going, from grip to give,
The narrow milky way in the black ice,

The race-up, the free passage and return—
It followed on itself like a ring of light
We knew we'd come through and kept sailing towards.

Scissor-and-slap abruptness of a latch.
Its coldness to the thumb. Its see-saw lift
And drop and innocent harshness.

Which is a music of binding and of loosing
Unheard in this generation, but there to be
Called up or called down at a touch renewed.

Once the latch pronounces, roof
Is original again, threshold fatal,
The sanction powerful as the foreboding.

Your footstep is already known, so bow
Just a little, raise your right hand,
Make impulse one with wilfulness, and enter.

x x x

On St Brigid's Day the new life could be entered
By going through her girdle of straw rope:
The proper way for men was right leg first,

Then right arm and right shoulder, head, then left
Shoulder, arm and leg. Women drew it down
Over the body and stepped out of it.

The open they came into by these moves
Stood opener, hoops came off the world,
They could feel the February air

Still soft above their heads and imagine
The limp rope fray and flare like wind-borne gleanings
Or an unhindered goldfinch over ploughland.

xxxi

Not an avenue and not a bower.
For a quarter-mile or so, where the county road
Is running straight across North Antrim bog,

Tall old fir trees line it on both sides.
Scotch firs, that is. Calligraphic shocks
Bushed and tufted in prevailing winds.

You drive into a meaning made of trees.
Or not exactly trees. It is a sense
Of running through and under without let,

Of glimpse and dapple. A life all trace and skim
The car has vanished out of. A fanned nape
Sensitive to the millionth of a flicker.

xxxii

Running water never disappointed.
Crossing water always furthered something.
Stepping stones were stations of the soul.

A kesh could mean the track some called a *causey*
Raised above the wetness of the bog,
Or the causey where it bridged old drains and streams.

It steadies me to tell these things. Also
I cannot mention keshes or the ford
Without my father's shade appearing to me

On a path towards sunset, eyeing spades and clothes
That turfcutters stowed perhaps or souls cast off
Before they crossed the log that spans the burn.

Be literal a moment. Recollect
Walking out on what had been emptied out
After he died, turning your back and leaving.

That morning, tiles were harder, windows colder,
The raindrops on the pane more scourged, the grass
Barer to the sky, more wind-harrowed,

Or so it seemed. The house that he had planned
'Plain, big, straight, ordinary, you know,'
A paradigm of rigour and correction,

Rebuke to fanciness and shrine to limit,
Stood firmer than ever for its own idea
Like a printed X-ray for the X-rayed body.

xxxiv

Yeats said, *To those who see spirits, human skin*
For a long time afterwards appears most coarse.
The face I see that all falls short of since

Passes down an aisle: I share the bus
From San Francisco Airport into Berkeley
With one other passenger, who's dropped

At the Treasure Island military base
Half-way across Bay Bridge. Vietnam-bound,
He could have been one of the newly dead come back,

Unsurprisable but still disappointed,
Having to bear his farmboy self again,
His shaving cuts, his otherworldly brow.

xxxv

Shaving cuts. The pallor of bad habits.
Sunday afternoons, when summer idled
And couples walked the road along the Foyle,

We brought a shaving mirror to our window
In the top storey of the boarders' dorms:
Lovers in the happy valley, cars

Eager-backed and silent, the absolute river
Between us and it all. We tilted the glass up
Into the sun and found the range and shone

A flitting light on what we could not have.
Brightness played over them in chancy sweeps
Like flashes from a god's shield or a dance-floor.

xxxvi

And yes, my friend, we too walked through a valley.
Once. In darkness. With all the streetlamps off.
As danger gathered and the march dispersed.

Scene from Dante, made more memorable
By one of his head-clearing similes—
Fireflies, say, since the policemen's torches

Clustered and flicked and tempted us to trust
Their unpredictable, attractive light.
We were like herded shades who had to cross

And did cross, in a panic, to the car
Parked as we'd left it, that gave when we got in
Like Charon's boat under the faring poets.

4. Squarings

In famous poems by the sage Han Shan,
Cold Mountain is a place that can also mean
A state of mind. Or different states of mind

At different times, for the poems seem
One-off, impulsive, the kind of thing that starts
I have sat here facing the Cold Mountain

For twenty-nine years, or *There is no path
That goes all the way*—enviable stuff,
Unfussy and believable.

Talking about it isn't good enough,
But quoting from it at least demonstrates
The virtue of an art that knows its mind.

We climbed the Capitol by moonlight, felt
The transports of temptation on the heights:
We were privileged and belated and we knew it.

Then something in me moved to prophesy
Against the beloved stand-offishness of marble
And all emulation of stone-cut verses.

'Down with form triumphant, long live,' said I,
'Form mendicant and convalescent. We attend
The comeback of pure water and the prayer-wheel.'

To which a voice replied, 'Of course we do.
But the others are in the Forum Café waiting,
Wondering where we are. What'll you have?'

xxxix

When you sat, far-eyed and cold, in the basalt throne
Of the 'wishing chair' at Giant's Causeway,
The small of your back made very solid sense.

Like a papoose at sap-time strapped to a maple tree,
You gathered force out of the world-tree's hardness.
If you stretched your hand forth, things might turn to
    stone.

But you were only goose-fleshed skin and bone,
The rocks and wonder of the world were only
Lava crystallized, salts of the earth

The wishing chair gave a savour to, its kelp
And ozone freshening your outlook
Beyond the range you thought you'd settled for.

x l

I was four but I turned four hundred maybe,
Encountering the ancient dampish feel
Of a clay floor. Maybe four thousand even.

Anyhow, there it was. Milk poured for cats
In a rank puddle-place, splash-darkened mould
Around the terracotta water-crock.

Ground of being. Body's deep obedience
To all its shifting tenses. A half-door
Opening directly into starlight.

Out of that earth house I inherited
A stack of singular, cold memory-weights
To load me, hand and foot, in the scale of things.

xli

Sand-bed, they said. And gravel-bed. Before
I knew river shallows or river pleasures
I knew the ore of longing in those words.

The places I go back to have not failed
But will not last. Waist-deep in cow-parsley,
I re-enter the swim, riding or quelling

The very currents memory is composed of,
Everything accumulated ever
As I took squarings from the tops of bridges

Or the banks of self at evening.
Lick of fear. Sweet transience. Flirt and splash.
Crumpled flow the sky-dipped willows trailed in.

xlii

Heather and kesh and turf stacks reappear
Summer by summer still, grasshoppers and all,
The same yet rarer: fields of the nearly blessed

Where gaunt ones in their shirtsleeves stooped and dug
Or stood alone at dusk surveying bog-banks—
Apparitions now, yet active still

And territorial, still sure of their ground,
Still interested, not knowing how far
The country of the shades has been pushed back,

How long the lark has stopped outside these fields
And only seems unstoppable to them
Caught like a far hill in a freak of sunshine.

xliii

Choose one set of tracks and track a hare
Until the prints stop, just like that, in snow.
End of the line. Smooth drifts. Where did she go?

Back on her tracks, of course, then took a spring
Yards off to the side; clean break; no scent or sign.
She landed in her form and ate the snow.

Consider too the ancient hieroglyph
Of 'hare and zigzag', which meant 'to exist',
To be on the *qui vive*, weaving and dodging

Like our friend who sprang (goodbye) beyond our ken
And missed a round at last (but of course he'd stood it):
The shake-the-heart, the dew-hammer, the far-eyed.

xliv

All gone into the world of light? Perhaps
As we read the line sheer forms do crowd
The starry vestibule. Otherwise

They do not. What lucency survives
Is blanched as worms on nightlines I would lift,
Ungratified if always well prepared

For the nothing there—which was only what had been
    there.
Although in fact it is more like a caught line snapping,
That moment of admission of *All gone,*

When the rod butt loses touch and the tip drools
And eddies swirl a dead leaf past in silence
Swifter (it seems) than the water's passage.

xlv

For certain ones what was written may come true:
They shall live on in the distance
At the mouths of rivers.

For our ones, no. They will re-enter
Dryness that was heaven on earth to them,
Happy to eat the scones baked out of clay.

For some, perhaps, the delta's reed-beds
And cold bright-footed seabirds always wheeling.
For our ones, snuff

And hob-soot and the heat off ashes.
And a judge who comes between them and the sun
In a pillar of radiant house-dust.

xlvi

Mountain air from the mountain up behind;
Out front, the end-of-summer, stone-walled fields;
And in a slated house the fiddle going

Like a flat stone skimmed at sunset
Or the irrevocable slipstream of flat earth
Still fleeing behind space.

Was music once a proof of God's existence?
As long as it admits things beyond measure,
That supposition stands.

So let the ear attend like a farmhouse window
In placid light, where the extravagant
Passed once under full sail into the longed-for.

xlvii

The visible sea at a distance from the shore
Or beyond the anchoring grounds
Was called the offing.

The emptier it stood, the more compelled
The eye that scanned it.
But once you turned your back on it, your back

Was suddenly all eyes like Argus's.
Then, when you'd look again, the offing felt
Untrespassed still, and yet somehow vacated

As if a lambent troop that exercised
On the borders of your vision had withdrawn
Behind the skyline to manoeuvre and regroup.

xlviii

Strange how things in the offing, once they're sensed,
Convert to things foreknown;
And how what's come upon is manifest

Only in light of what has been gone through.
Seventh heaven may be
The whole truth of a sixth sense come to pass.

At any rate, when light breaks over me
The way it did on the road beyond Coleraine
Where wind got saltier, the sky more hurried

And silver lamé shivered on the Bann
Out in mid-channel between the painted poles,
That day I'll be in step with what escaped me.

The Crossing

(*Inferno*, Canto III, lines 82–129)

And there in a boat that came heading towards us
Was an old man, his hair snow-white with age,
Raging and bawling, 'Woe to you, wicked spirits!

Oh, never hope to see the heavenly skies!
I come to bring you to the other shore,
To eternal darkness, to the fire and ice.

And you there, you, the living soul, separate
Yourself from these others who are dead.'
But when he saw that I did not stand aside

He said, 'By another way, by other harbours
You shall reach a different shore and pass over.
A lighter boat must be your carrier.'

And my guide said, 'Quiet your anger, Charon.
There where all can be done that has been willed
This has been willed; so there can be no question.'

Then straightaway he shut his grizzled jaws,
The ferryman of that livid marsh,
Who had wheels of fire flaming round his eyes.

But as soon as they had heard the cruel words,
Those lost souls, all naked and exhausted,
Changed their colour and their teeth chattered;

They blasphemed God and their parents on the earth,
The human race, the place and date and seedbed
Of their own begetting and of their birth,

Then all together, bitterly weeping, made
Their way towards the accursed shore that waits
For every man who does not fear his God.

The demon Charon's eyes are like hot coals fanned.
He beckons them and herds all of them in
And beats with his oar whoever drops behind.

As one by one the leaves fall off in autumn
Until at last the branch is bare and sees
All that was looted from it on the ground,

So the bad seed of Adam, at a signal
Pitch themselves off that shore one by one,
Each like a falcon answering its call.

They go away like this over the brown waters
And before they have landed on the other side
Upon this side once more a new crowd gathers.

'My son,' the courteous master said to me,
'All those who die under the wrath of God
Come together here from every country

And they are eager to go across the river
Because Divine Justice goads them with its spur
So that their fear is turned into desire.

No good spirits ever pass this way
And therefore, if Charon objects to you,
You should understand well what his words imply.'